FOUNDATIONS OF PHYSICS

MAGNETISM

by Anita Nahta Amin

I0902167

pogo

Ideas for Parents and Teachers

Pogo Books let children practice reading informational text while introducing them to nonfiction features such as headings, labels, sidebars, maps, and diagrams, as well as a table of contents, glossary, and index.

Carefully leveled text with a strong photo match offers early fluent readers the support they need to succeed.

Before Reading

- "Walk" through the book and point out the various nonfiction features. Ask the student what purpose each feature serves.
- Look at the glossary together. Read and discuss the words.

Read the Book

- Have the child read the book independently.
- Invite him or her to list questions that arise from reading.

After Reading

- Discuss the child's questions. Talk about how he or she might find answers to those questions.
- Prompt the child to think more. Ask: How do you use magnetism?

Pogo Books are published by Jump!
5357 Penn Avenue South
Minneapolis, MN 55419
www.jumplibrary.com

Library of Congress Cataloging-in-Publication Data

Names: Amin, Anita Nahta, author.
Title: Magnetism / by Anita Nahta Amin.
Description: Minneapolis, MN: Jump!, Inc., [2022]
Series: Foundations of physics
Includes index. | Audience: Ages 7-10
Identifiers: LCCN 2021008036 (print)
LCCN 2021008037 (ebook)
ISBN 9781636900421 (hardcover)
ISBN 9781636900438 (paperback)
ISBN 9781636900445 (ebook)
Subjects: LCSH: Magnetism–Juvenile literature.
Magnets–Juvenile literature.
Classification: LCC QC753.7 .A45 2022 (print)
LCC QC753.7 (ebook) | DDC 538–dc23
LC record available at https://lccn.loc.gov/2021008036
LC ebook record available at https://lccn.loc.gov/2021008037

Editor: Eliza Leahy
Designer: Michelle Sonnek

Photo Credits: New Africa/Shutterstock, cover, 19; revers/Shutterstock, 1; Shutterstock, 3, 4, 18; streetfotolab/Shutterstock, 5; BanksPhotos/iStock, 6-7; Ju Jae-young/Shutterstock, 8-9; WIN12_ET/Shutterstock, 10-11; noisuk Photo/Shutterstock, 12; H.S. Photos/Alamy, 13; Markus Mainka/Shutterstock, 14-15; Nazarova Mariia/Shutterstock, 16-17; iJeab/Shutterstock, 20-21; mohamadhafizmohamad/Shutterstock, 23.

Printed in the United States of America at Corporate Graphics in North Mankato, Minnesota.

TABLE OF CONTENTS

CHAPTER 1

HOW DO MAGNETS WORK?

A photo sticks to the refrigerator. The refrigerator door seals shut. What do these have in common? They use magnets!

Magnets are metals that **attract** certain other kinds of metal. They can also **repel**. This pull or push **force** is called magnetism.

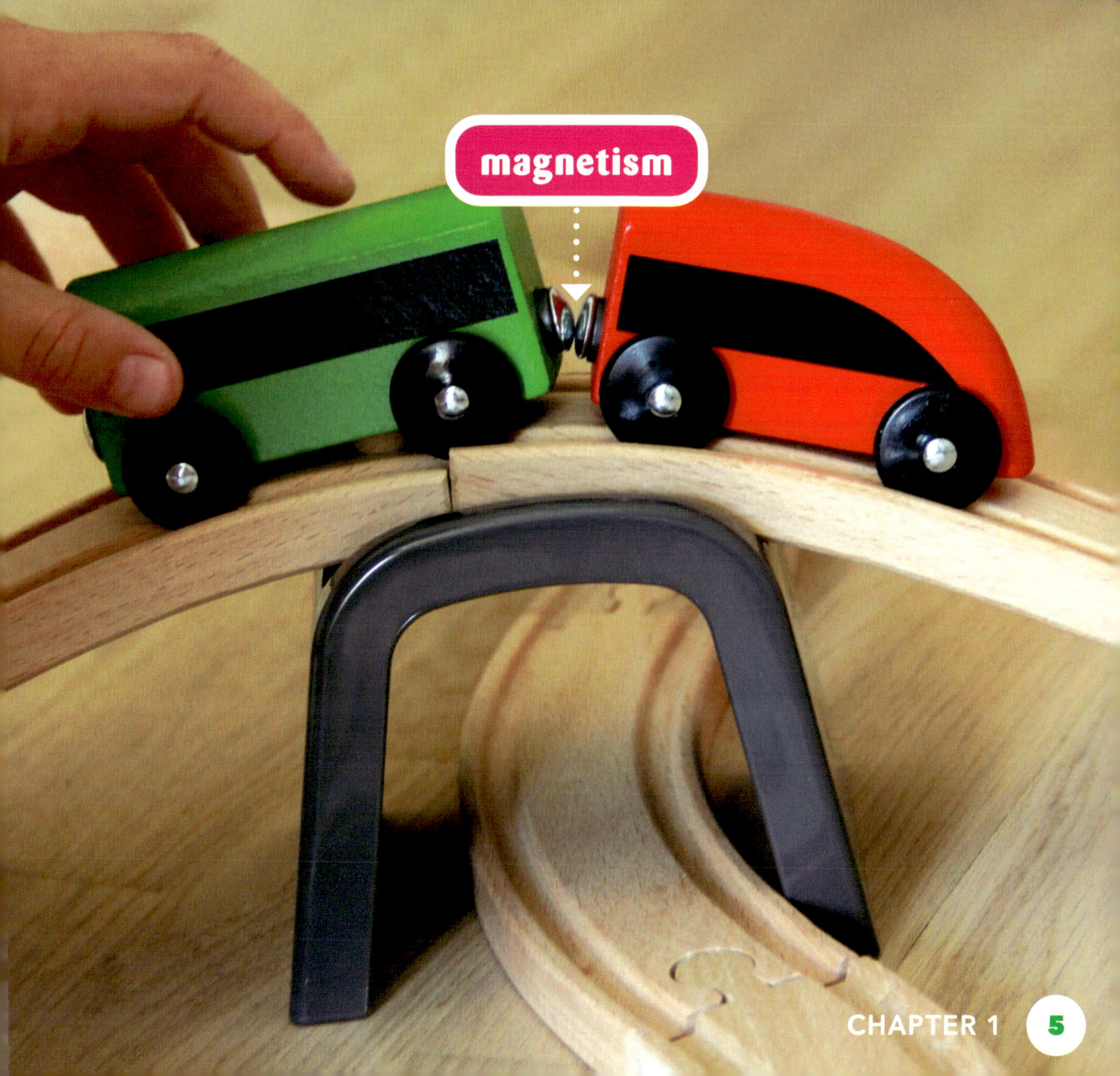

magnet

Magnets stick to metal objects, such as lockers and cars. They also stick to some rocks. Why? These also have magnetic metals, such as iron and nickel.

DID YOU KNOW?

Some magnets are so strong they can lift cars! These magnets are used on cranes to move cars.

All objects are made of **atoms**. Atoms have **charges** that spin. This makes an **electric current**. The electric current forms a **magnetic field** around each atom. These fields are where magnetism is at work.

In magnetic objects, the fields add up. They make one big magnetic field.

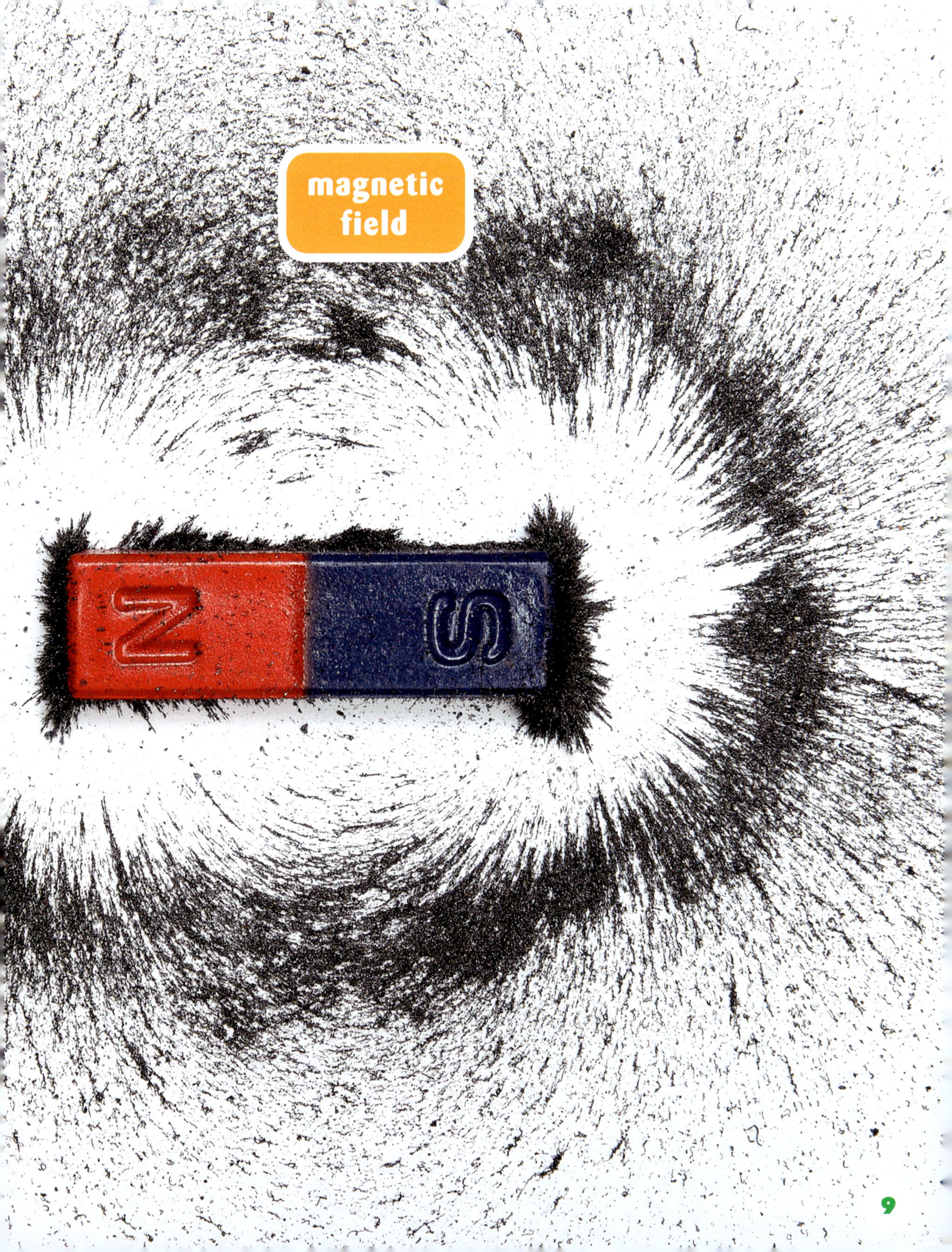
magnetic field
N
S

A magnet does not have to touch an object for magnetism to work. The object just has to be in the magnet's field. What happens if they get close? The magnet's force on the object gets stronger.

DID YOU KNOW?

You can test this with a refrigerator magnet. How? Hold the magnet a few inches away from the refrigerator door. Slowly move it closer. Do you feel the force get stronger?

CHAPTER 2

ATTRACT AND REPEL

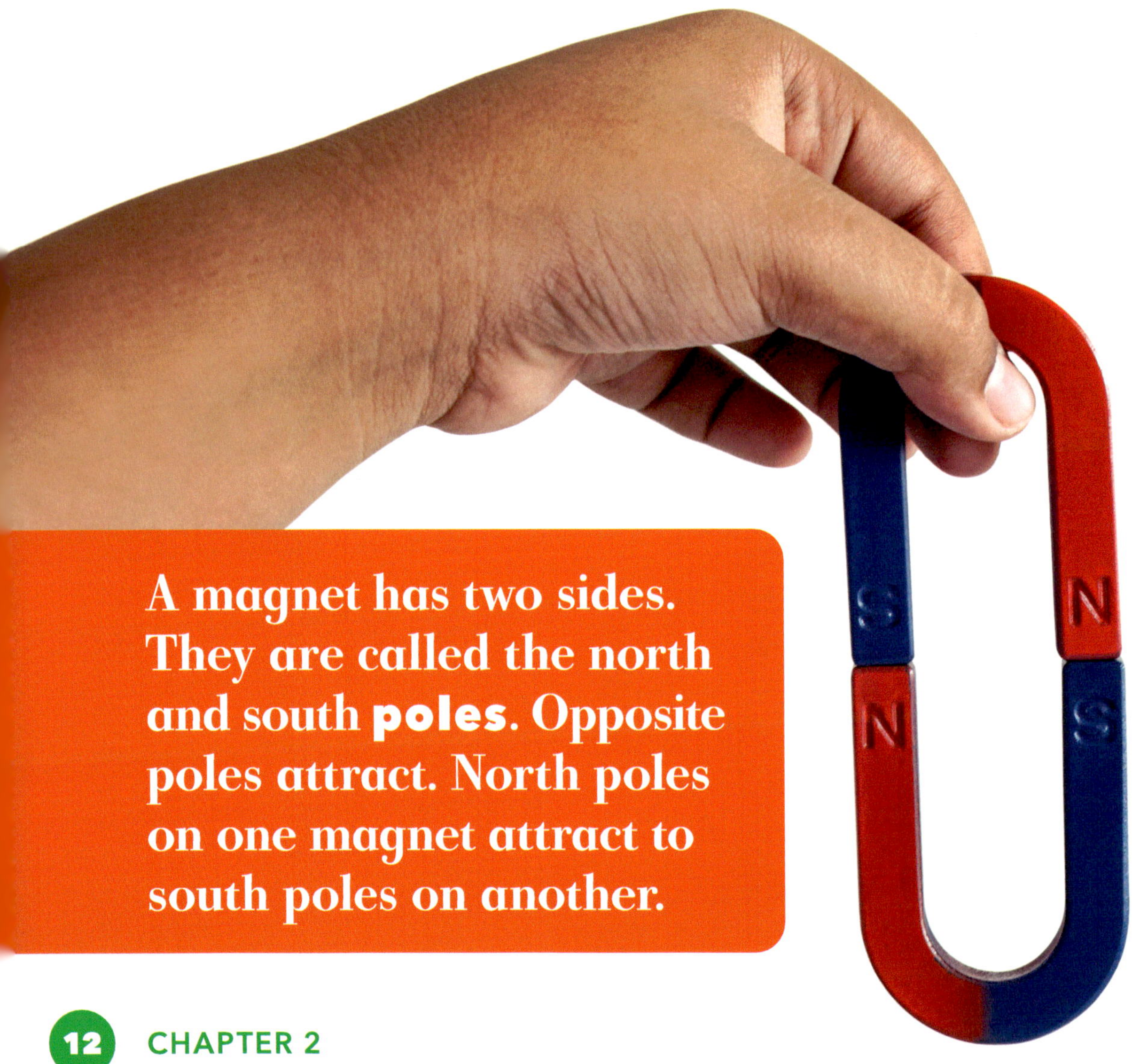

A magnet has two sides. They are called the north and south **poles**. Opposite poles attract. North poles on one magnet attract to south poles on another.

Same poles repel. North poles of different magnets push each other away. South poles do the same.

maglev
train

This is how a **maglev** train works. The train and track have magnets. The same kind of poles face each other. They repel one another. This causes the train to lift. It floats above the tracks.

Did you know Earth is a magnet? It has liquid iron in it. This makes an electric current. The current makes a magnetic field around Earth. This field is what attracts the magnet in a **compass**.

TAKE A LOOK!

The south end of Earth's magnet attracts the north end of a compass's magnet. Take a look!

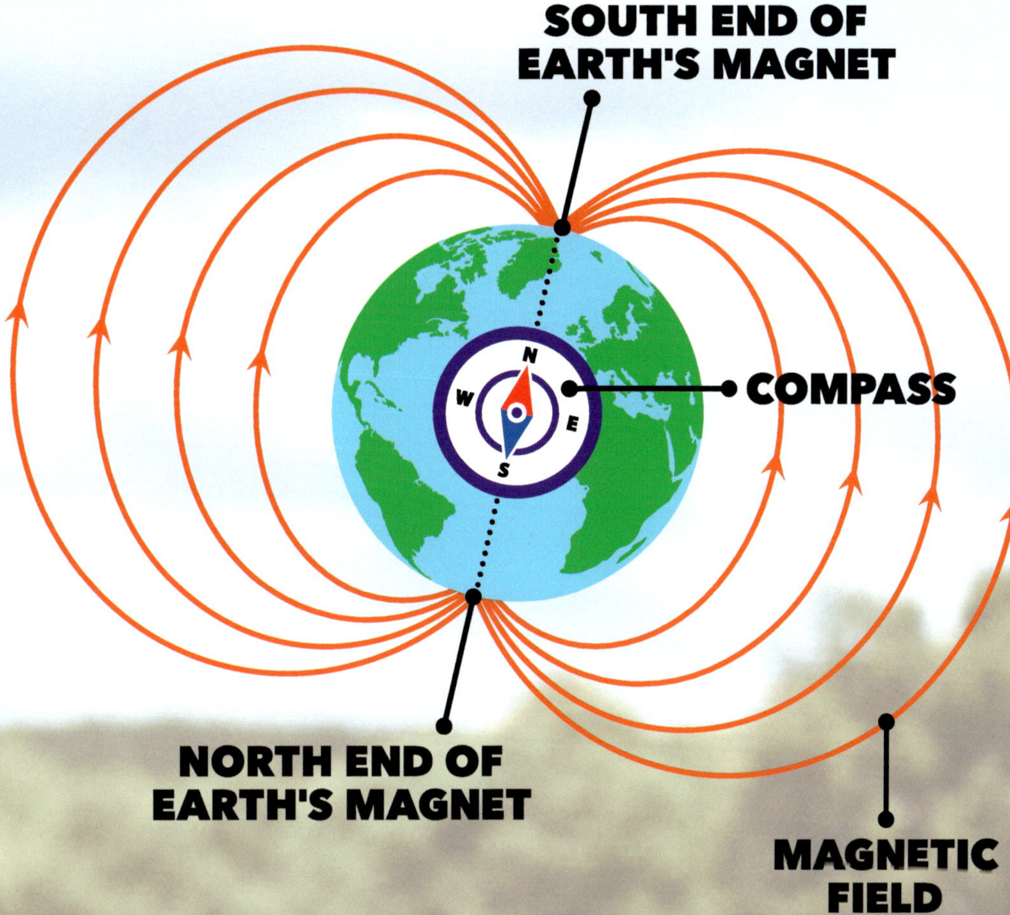

CHAPTER 3

KINDS OF MAGNETS

There are three kinds of magnets. **Permanent** magnets stay on. Their magnetic force stays busy. Refrigerator magnets are one example.

An object can turn into a **temporary** magnet. A paper clip is one example. These kind of magnets have to start out in another magnet's field. Some stay magnetized only while they are in the field. Some stay magnetized for years after the field goes away.

Electromagnets have metal centers. They are coils of wire. Electric currents run through the wire. A magnetic field forms around the wire. These magnets are in headphones and computers.

Magnetism helps us every day! Where else do you see this force at work?

DID YOU KNOW?

Magnets can even attract food! How? Some cereals have iron.

ACTIVITIES & TOOLS

TRY THIS!

MAKE TEMPORARY MAGNETS

See which household items can become magnets with this fun activity!

What You Need:

- two paper clips
- a magnet
- coins

1. **Leave a paper clip on a magnet for five minutes. Did the paper clip stick to the magnet?**
2. **Take the paper clip off the magnet.**
3. **Gently rub the paper clip on the second paper clip. Did the first paper clip turn into a magnet and attract the second paper clip? Why do you think this happens?**
4. **Repeat Steps 1 through 3 but leave the paper clip on the magnet for one hour instead. Is it easier to pick up the second paper clip now?**
5. **Try Steps 1 through 4 with coins instead of paper clips. Does the coin become a magnet?**
6. **Try other items instead of paper clips or coins. Some items may take longer than others to become magnetic. Which items become magnets? Which items do not? Why do you think this is the case?**

GLOSSARY

atoms: The tiniest parts of elements that have all the properties of their elements.

attract: To cause something to move closer or touch.

charges: The parts of atoms that make things stick or push away.

compass: An instrument with a magnetic pointer that always points north and that is used for finding directions.

electric current: The flow of charge from atom to atom.

force: Any action that produces, stops, or changes the shape or movement of an object.

maglev: Short for magnetic levitation; a system of high-speed train transportation in which the train uses powerful magnets to float above the track.

magnetic field: The area around a magnet or electric current that has the power to attract other metals.

permanent: Lasting or meant to last a long time.

poles: The two opposite ends of magnets.

repel: To push back.

temporary: Lasting only a short time.

INDEX

TO LEARN MORE

Finding more information is as easy as 1, 2, 3.

1. Go to www.factsurfer.com
2. Enter "magnetism" into the search box.
3. Choose your book to see a list of websites.

FACT SURFER